Stories from the Storyteller™

# The Mighty Miracles of Jesus

Jonathan Evans
Illustrations by Todd Hampson

Harvest Kids
Harvest House Publishers
Eugene, Oregon

The Scriptures from Matthew are paraphrased.
Luke 5:4-7 is quoted from the ESV® Bible (The Holy Bible, English Standard Version®), copyright © 2001 by Crossway, a publishing ministry of Good News Publishers. Used with permission. All rights reserved. The ESV text may not be quoted in any publication made available to the public by a Creative Commons license. The ESV may not be translated in whole or in part into any other language.

Illustrations by Todd Hampson
Cover design by Bryce Williamson
Interior design by Chad Dougherty
Other images © Mashot / Getty Images
Evans family photo by Joshua Farris, PharrisPhotos.com

For bulk, special sales, or ministry purchases, please call 1-800-547-8979.
Email: CustomerService@hhpbooks.com

STORIES FROM THE STORYTELLER is a trademark of eLegacy Venture, LLC.

This logo is a federally registered trademark of The Hawkins Children's LLC. Harvest House Publishers, Inc., is the exclusive licensee of the trademark.

Based on the Stories from the Storyteller™ video series, produced by Jonathan and Kanika Evans.

The QR codes on pages 4, 23, 42, 61, and 64 link to videos that are also available at these URLs:

https://tonyevans.org/storytellermiraclesintro
https://tonyevans.org/storytellermiracles1
https://tonyevans.org/storytellermiracles2
https://tonyevans.org/storytellermiracles3
https://tonyevans.org/storytellermiraclesoutro

For questions regarding the QR codes, URLs, or videos, please visit tonyevans.org/contact.

**The Mighty Miracles of Jesus**

Published by Harvest House Publishers
Eugene, Oregon 97408
www.harvesthousepublishers.com

ISBN 978-0-7369-8577-2 (hardcover)

Library of Congress Control Number: 2025935605



**Printed in China**

25 26 27 28 29 30 31 32 33 / RDS / 10 9 8 7 6 5 4 3 2 1

# Contents

# Introduction

**HELLO, PARENTS,** and thank you for using this book to help teach your kids stories from the Storyteller. This book focuses on a few of the mighty miracles of Jesus, the Son of God. We want your kids to be **begging for bedtime,** so we suggest reading a chapter to your children each night and then using the QR code provided so they can watch a bonus video on your device after each story is read from the book. We hope you enjoy *The Mighty Miracles of Jesus!*

To scan the QR code at the end of each chapter:

1. Open the camera on your phone or tablet.
2. Aim it at the QR code.
3. Tap the banner that appears.

1

# Walking on Chaos

# NO MORE

The Evans kids were all ready to go to the pool.

"Summer is officially here! Chillin' by the pool. Hanging out with friends. I love summer!" Kelsey proclaimed.

# SCHOOL!

"Best of all, NO MORE SCHOOL!" they shouted in unison.

Just as the kids were about to walk out the door, their mom entered the room and said, "Sorry guys, summer isn't here just yet. J2 still has a project to do."

"NOOOOOO!" they shouted.

Just then, J2 walked into the room.

"Did someone say my name?" he asked.

Mrs. Evans explained that he had a science experiment that he hadn't completed because of a soccer game. His brother and sisters were unhappy with him, as they were ready for their summer break.

Everyone gathered around a paper-mache volcano.

"This is a timed science experiment. You have one minute to read and follow the instructions. Ready, set, go!" Mrs. Evans shouted.

J2 frantically picked up the paper instructions and began to read aloud, "Step one. Four tablespoons of baking soda."

"In the pantry!" Kelsey shouted.

J2 quickly ran to the pantry and brought back a box.

"That's baking powder, not baking soda!" Kelsey yelled.

"What's the difference?" J2 asked.

Kelsey loved to talk about baking and perked up, "Well, baking soda will create a coarse, chewy cookie texture, while baking powder will give baked goods—"

"Not now, Kelsey!" shouted Kam.

J2 quickly ran back to the pantry and returned with baking soda. He put the four tablespoons in the volcano and picked up the instructions.

"Step two. One tablespoon of dish soap," he read aloud.

J2 quickly returned with the dish soap from the kitchen and put the right amount into the volcano.

"Summer is so close, yet so far away," whined Kam.

J2 read, "Step three. One cup of vinegar."

"Fifteen seconds!" Mrs. Evans called out.

"Fifteen seconds! I can't do it," exclaimed J2.

"J2, just focus on the steps, not the clock," coached Mrs. Evans.

A look of determination grew over J2's face. He sprinted across the kitchen and returned in a flash. He measured out the cup of vinegar and poured it into the volcano.

"Five seconds!" Mrs. Evans warned.

The kids began to count down, “Four. Three. Two…”

And just as the kids said “one,” the volcano erupted.

“Congratulations, J2. You’ve completed your final science project,” Mrs. Evans announced.

Everyone cheered, “Yay! Summer can officially begin!”

After a long day at the pool, the Evans family returned to their house, put on their superhero pajamas, and piled onto Mr. and Mrs. Evans's bed.

"I was reminded of a story today when J2 was scrambling to finish his science project, and you guys thought summer was doomed," Mrs. Evans said.

"I definitely thought summer was doomed," Kam remembered.

"Me too," added Bunny.

"Well, Peter and the disciples thought they were doomed too. In the book of Matthew, the disciples were out on a small boat when big waves began to toss the boat around, and they thought they were—"

"Doooomed!" Bunny exclaimed.

"That's right, Bunny. But then they saw Jesus approaching in the distance, walking on the water, and they became even more terrified," Mrs. Evans shared.

"Whoa!" shouted Kam.

Mrs. Evans continued, "Then Jesus said to them, 'Take courage! It is I. Don't be afraid.' Peter got out of the boat and began to walk on the water toward Jesus. But shortly after getting out of the boat, he took his eyes off Jesus and began to sink. Jesus pulled him up and saved him."

"Why do you guys think Peter began to sink?" Mr. Evans asked.

"I think Peter began to think about the storm and what would happen to him rather than putting his faith in Jesus to protect him," J2 answered.

"Exactly, J2. He let his fear get in the way of his faith. You know there will be scary and intense times in life, but we don't have to be afraid. We need to keep our focus on Jesus. He promises to walk with us through any storm.

And if we do take our eyes off Him, we can call out to Jesus, and He'll pull us up again," Mr. Evans said.

Bunny looked at Tyson sitting in his duckie float and commanded, "Tyson, get out of that boat!"

Suddenly, Bunny jumped off the bed, landing on the edge of the float and launching Tyson high into the air.

Mr. Evans laughed, "Well, that's one way to get him out of the boat!"

2

# Kelsey's Kookie Kitchen

Kelsey's friends were coming over for her annual Kelsey's Kookie Kitchen party, and there wasn't much time to decorate.

"Listen up, everyone, we don't have much time. Mom, Kylar, and Kam—you are on tablecloths and snacks. Tyson, J2, and Bunny—you guys are on streamers and balloons. Dad, I need you to go to the grocery store," she demanded.

"Uh huh," Mr. Evans responded as he read his book.

Mrs. Evans, Kam, and Kylar spread out cups and plates onto a bright yellow tablecloth.

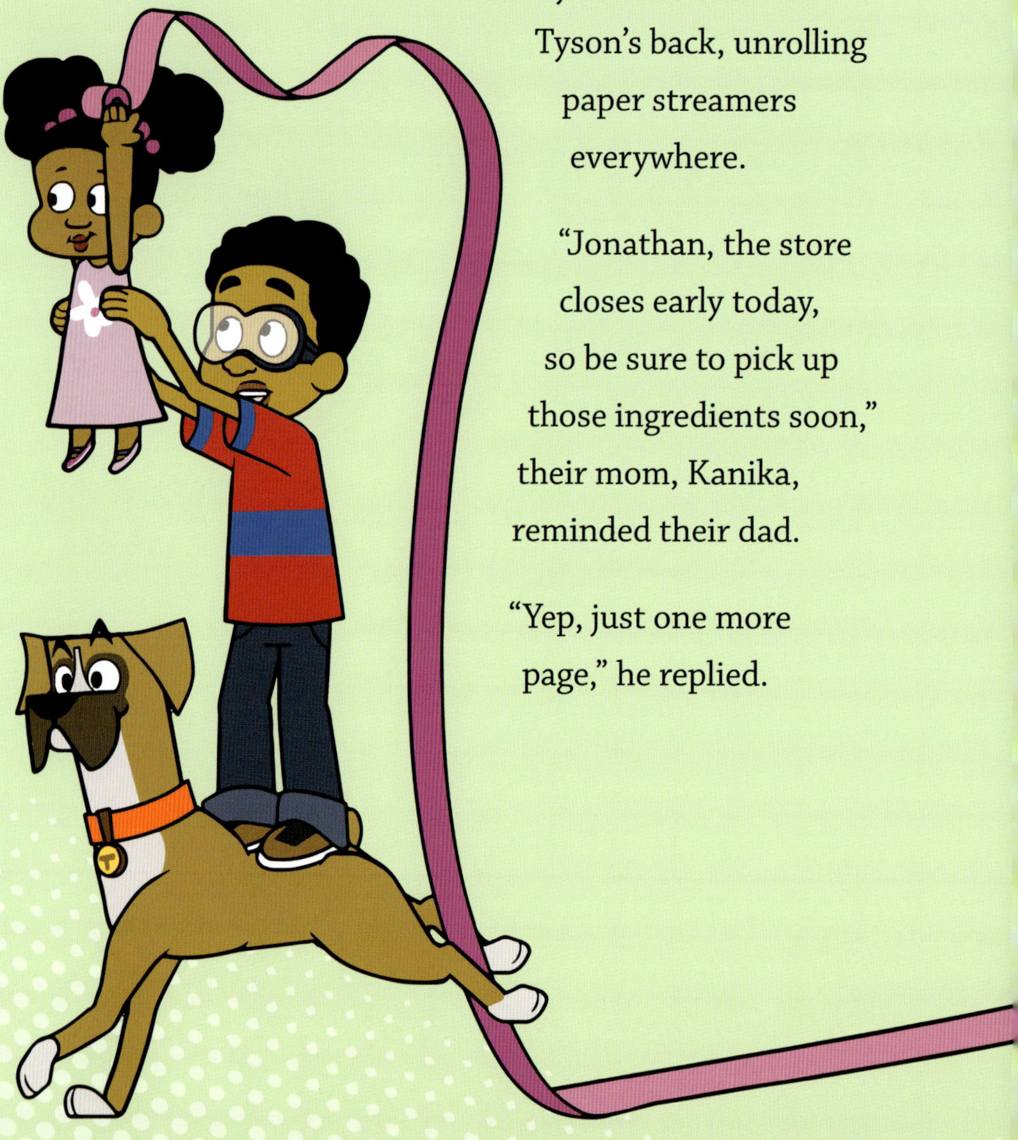

Bunny and J2 rode on Tyson's back, unrolling paper streamers everywhere.

"Jonathan, the store closes early today, so be sure to pick up those ingredients soon," their mom, Kanika, reminded their dad.

"Yep, just one more page," he replied.

By the time Tyson, J2, and Bunny were done, everything—including Dad—was covered in paper streamers.

A few hours later, the decorations were complete, and Kelsey's friends began to arrive.

"I can't wait to see what kind of cookie you create this year!" Ellie exclaimed.

"Hey, Dad, can you bring out those ingredients from the grocery store?" requested Kelsey.

"Ingredients?" he asked. Mr. Evans suddenly realized he never went to the grocery store. "I'm so sorry, Kelsey," he apologized.

"What am I going to do now?" Kelsey demanded.

"Here are three granola bars from my sneaky snacker stash," Kylar offered.

Kam handed Kelsey some graham crackers. "I traded my carrots for these five graham crackers at school yesterday," he stated.

"What kind of cookie can I make with five graham crackers and three granola bars?" Kelsey whined.

"Kelsey, I know you're frustrated, but we can still be thankful for what we have," her mom replied.

Kelsey walked into the kitchen and peered into the pantry, feeling defeated.

"Lord, I don't know what to do. My friends are excited to see this year's cookie creation. I really need Your help here, Lord," she prayed.

While looking at the various ingredients on the pantry shelf, she began to devise a plan.

"Applesauce. I could use that! Cinnamon. Perfect!" Kelsey thought.

She grabbed all the ingredients and ran back to the party.

“Kelsey’s Kookie Kitchen is back!” Kelsey proclaimed.

Everyone cheered as she began to prep.

"Tyson, bring me three cups of flour. Bunny, I need a half cup of applesauce. J2, set the oven to 350 degrees and butter up the cookie sheet," requested Kelsey.

Kelsey crushed, poured, mixed, whipped, and blended all her ingredients, including the graham crackers and granola bars. She carefully scooped out even dollops of dough onto the cookie sheet and slipped the trays into the oven.

A few minutes later, Kelsey brought out a plate of warm cookies.

"I hope you like them," she offered with uncertainty.

Everyone smiled and took a cookie off the plate. Their eyes lit up as they chewed.

"These are amazing!" Ellie announced.

Kelsey couldn't believe what she was hearing! Everyone loved the cookies so much that they wanted seconds and thirds.

Later that day, after all the partygoers had gone home, a few cookies remained.

"Dad, would you like a cookie? There is just enough for each of us to have one," Kelsey observed.

"I feel badly for letting you down today, Kelsey, so you deserve to eat my cookie," Mr. Evans responded.

As Kelsey hugged her dad, he announced, "Well, it's about time for—"

"Storytime!" they all shouted in unison.

With everyone in bed wearing their superhero pajamas, Mrs. Evans began reading from the book of Matthew, chapter 14.

"Jesus and His disciples were with thousands of people who had followed Jesus to a remote area, and they were too far away from town to get food.

A disciple approached Jesus with five loaves of bread and two fish. Jesus prayed over the food and gave thanks for it."

"That's not much food for thousands of people," observed Kam.

"Not nearly enough, Kam. But after Jesus prayed, He began to break up the food for the disciples to hand out to the people. And guess what?" Mr. Evans inquired.

"What?" Bunny asked.

"Everyone ate until they were full, and they still had twelve baskets full of leftover bread and fish!" he exclaimed.

"You know, I was stressed when I saw so few ingredients for the party. But after I prayed about it, Jesus showed me that I had more than I thought," agreed Kelsey.

Kelsey's dad was proud of her for leaning on Jesus for help. He responded, "God knows what we need. And when we are thankful and trust Him with the little we have, He blesses us with even more."

Everyone looked over to see Bunny praying with two fish crackers in her hand.

"What are you doing, Bunny?" questioned Kam.

"Praying for more fishies!" she announced.

The Evans family giggled as Bunny prayed over her crackers.

3

# The Great Catch

One day while the Evans family was hanging out in the living room, Kelsey opened Storygram on her phone and posted a picture of herself.

"I think these shoes are my color. What do you think?" Kelsey typed.

Kelsey looked down at her phone screen, waiting for someone to respond to her post.

"Ugh! No one follows me," Kelsey proclaimed.

"Your mom and I have followers," Mr. Evans shared.

Kelsey was shocked to hear this and quickly opened her parents' Storygram page and watched a video of them at a basketball court.

Kanika and Jonathan are looking at the camera. "Join us next time as we continue to learn how to dive deep with Jesus!" Jonathan shared.

"And I'll show you my famous hook shot," laughed Kanika.

Kelsey stopped the video. "Wow, you guys have tons of followers."

“J2 and I have followers too,” added Kam.

Kelsey opened their Storygram page and watched a video of her brothers.

“Hey, everyone, this is Kam and J2,” Kam stated.

"We'll show you some cool moves on our God and Games channel!" announced J2.

Kelsey was again shocked at their number of followers.

"How do you all have so many followers, and I only have a few?" Kelsey questioned.

Kelsey's dad picked up her phone. "Let's take a look at what you're posting."

He flipped through posts of Kelsey talking about new wardrobes, hairstyles, and her love of pizza.

"I think I see why you don't have followers, Kelsey," observed Mr. Evans.

"Please tell me!" Kelsey begged.

"These posts are all about you, and honestly, they're shallow," her dad replied.

"They're shallow?" she asked, perplexed.

"Yep!" everyone responded.

"Kelsey, did you notice on our Storygram page how we use our gifts to share about Jesus? The Lord wants us to use the special gifts He's given us to tell the world about His love and grace," Mr. Evans proclaimed.

"I mean, I want to tell people about Jesus, too, but what is my special gift?" Kelsey wondered.

"You're so creative, Kelsey. I'm sure the Lord will help you figure it out," responded J2.

Later that day, Kelsey was in her room, sitting at her crafting desk. She began to talk to Jesus out loud.

"They are right, Lord. You did make me creative. I love that You made me that way," acknowledged Kelsey.

She picked up a piece of paper and scissors and began to cut shapes out of the paper.

Kelsey continued to pray aloud, "When I create things, I'm reminded of how creative You are, God. You created every kind of bird, tree, and flower. You even created color! Thanks for inventing pink, by the way.

When I'm being creative, I feel close to You, Jesus. And I feel like You are close to me," Kelsey prayed.

Kelsey set the scissors down and opened the paper to reveal a paper cutout of a tree with birds.

"Wow!" Kam exclaimed.

Kelsey turned around to find her family watching her. Mrs. Evans had been filming her the whole time.

"That was amazing, Kelsey. I think you should post this," Mrs. Evans said.

Kelsey reluctantly agreed, and within minutes, her post was blowing up with hearts and great comments. She was amazed at the positive response to her sharing her love for God through her creativity.

Later that evening, the kids put on their superhero pajamas for storytime and piled onto their parents' bed.

Mr. Evans began to read from Luke chapter 5 when Jesus was teaching a crowd from a boat. "And when he had finished speaking, he said to Simon, 'Put out into the deep and let down your nets for a catch.'

And Simon answered, 'Master, we toiled all night and took nothing! But at your word I will let down the nets.' And when they had done this, they enclosed a large number of fish, and their nets were breaking. They signaled to their partners in the other boat to come and help them. And they came and filled both the boats, so they began to sink."

"Peter was discouraged, just like I was," Kelsey observed.

"That's right, Kelsey, and Jesus instructed him to go deep. Let's get away from being shallow and focusing only on ourselves. Instead, let's follow Jesus and let Him use us through the gifts He's given us to draw followers to Himself," Mr. Evans encouraged.

The next day, Kelsey set up her camera in front of her crafting desk and began to record herself.

“Hi, everyone! Have you ever thought about how much God loves you? Well, today I have a very special project for us to do together. So follow me as we discover God’s big and endless love for us. Are you ready?” Kelsey asked with a big smile.

**Jonathan Evans** is a mentor, author, speaker, and former NFL fullback. He treasures his relationship with Christ, using his life to glorify God and impact people by equipping and encouraging them in their faith.

A graduate of Dallas Theological Seminary with a master's degree in Christian leadership, Jonathan serves as the lead pastor of Oak Cliff Bible Fellowship, where his father, Dr. Tony Evans, served as senior pastor for 48 years. Jonathan has authored several books, including *Your Time Is Now* and *Fighting Your Battles*. He also teamed up with his father to write *Get in the Game*, a practical guidebook filled with sports analogies and spiritual truths aimed at empowering readers with the skills they need to live victoriously.

Following his NFL career, Jonathan now serves as the chaplain of the Dallas Cowboys. He and his wife, Kanika, are the proud parents of Kelsey, Jonathan II, Kamden, Kylar, and Jade Wynter. They reside in Dallas, Texas.

**Todd Hampson** (MBTS, Dallas Theological Seminary) is a speaker, illustrator, animation producer, and the author of The Non-Prophet's Guide™ book series. He is also a cohost on the *Prophecy Pros Podcast* alongside Jeff Kinley. Todd's award-winning animation company, Timbuktoons, has produced content for many well-known ministry organizations. He and his wife are the proud parents of three grown children (and one daughter-in-law) and make their home in Georgia. ToddHampson.com